Winning Ways

Understanding Preschoolers

Gigi Schweikert

Name: _____

Date: _____

Redleaf Press®
www.redleafpress.org
800-423-8309

Also in the Winning Ways series by Gigi Schweikert
> *Being a Professional*
> *Partnering with Families*
> *Becoming a Team Player*
> *Being a Supervisor*
> *Understanding Infants*
> *Understanding Toddlers and Twos*
> *Supporting Positive Behavior*
> *Responding to Behavior*
> *Guiding Challenging Behavior*

Published by Redleaf Press
10 Yorkton Court
St. Paul, MN 55117
www.redleafpress.org

First edition 2013
Cover design by Jim Handrigan
Cover photograph © Rob Hainer/Veer
Interior design by Erin Kirk New
Photograph on page 4 by Amal Ayoub
All other photographs by Steve Wewerka
Printed in the United States of America

Library of Congress Cataloging-in-Publication Data
Schweikert, Gigi, 1962-
   Winning ways for early childhood professionals. Understanding preschoolers /
 Gigi Schweikert.
     p. cm.
   ISBN 978-1-60554-137-2 (alk. paper)
   1. Education, Preschool—United States. 2. Preschool children—Development.
 3. Preschool children—Care.   I. Title. II. Title: Understanding preschoolers.
 LB1140.23.S36 2013
 372.210973—dc23
                          2012032001

Printed on acid-free paper   U18-04

Contents

From the Desk of Gigi Schweikert

Dear Winning Ways Reader
(and Preschool Teacher),

I absolutely love being a teacher. These days I teach mostly adults who teach children. Teaching is something I never tire of and always find exciting, and I completely lose all sense of time when I'm in the classroom or speaking at a conference. There's nothing I would rather do. Do you feel the same way?

That's me doing what I love most, working with children.

Earlier in my career, I spent many years teaching preschoolers at the United Nations Child Care Centre in New York City. The children in my class were from all over the world. Although the preschoolers were each unique in appearance, language, culture, and temperament, what was most interesting to me was that despite those significant differences, their approach to learning, their interactions with the world and others, and their joy of life were strikingly similar. They all loved to run on the playground. They all loved to play in water. They all loved books. They all loved to learn. They were all preschoolers.

Although English was our primary language, many times the children didn't speak the same language, but they played alongside one another just the same and always giggled at the same things. In my experience, preschool development is pretty universal.

Whether you're new to the field or a veteran preschool teacher of many years, I think you'll find the information in this Winning Ways book, *Understanding Preschoolers*, helpful. You'll learn a few things—I did during my research—and you'll be reminded of how important your job as an early childhood professional really is: helping all preschoolers you work with to learn and grow and be the best they can be.

After you finish reading *Understanding Preschoolers*, please send me your own thoughts, ideas, and stories about working with preschoolers at www.gigischweikert.com. I'd love to hear from you.

Children deserve our winning ways,

Introduction

What's the *Understanding Preschoolers* Workbook All About?

Welcome to the Winning Ways book *Understanding Preschoolers*. This book is one of three in the continuing series that includes *Understanding Infants, Understanding Toddlers and Twos,* and *Understanding Preschoolers.* You can read all three or work with the one that best equips you as an early childhood professional. The workbook is designed to help you

- Develop a better understanding of the growth and development of preschoolers

- Improve your interactions with preschoolers

- Help you create a more preschooler-appropriate routine and program

- Appreciate preschoolers and their unique personalities and temperaments

Who Are Preschoolers?

For the purpose of this book, preschoolers are children from three to five years of age, not yet ready for kindergarten but excited about learning. Some schools group preschoolers according to age, such as threes and fours, and others mix age groups. The fours are often known as *PK*, which stands for prekindergarten. However you group preschoolers, they are eager to explore. Preschoolers can better express their needs—compared with toddlers and twos—given their greater command of language, but they are still struggling to gain self-control. They need clear, simple rules to understand boundaries.

They have rich fantasy play and imagination and can even confuse fantasy with reality. I heard a preschooler once respond to another preschooler, "Yes, I will pretend I am a horse, if I can change back." Are you ready to learn more about understanding preschoolers? They will surprise you.

Who Should Read and Use the *Understanding Preschoolers* Workbook?

Understanding Preschoolers is intended for anyone who works with or is thinking about working with preschoolers and anyone who works with adults who work with preschoolers:

Veteran Educators Those who never tire of being with preschoolers, have been preschool teachers for life, and can honestly claim, "I love them all," even the ones about whom most of us give a little sigh of relief when they are absent.

New Teachers Those of you who have just started working with preschoolers and often question, especially in the midst of the children constantly yelling your name and running about with endless energy, "What am I doing here?"

Career Seekers Those who are considering becoming preschool teachers. The early childhood field needs trained, enthusiastic, active individuals to care for and educate preschoolers.

College Students Adult students in early childhood programs in colleges and universities.

Trainers Early childhood professionals facilitating seminars and workshops.

Professors Academics teaching adult students in early childhood programs in colleges and universities.

Program Supervisors Directors and other administrators who want to better support and train the staff in their preschool programs.

Stressed-Out Teachers Those of you who are burning out or giving in and need new ideas and encouragement for your preschool programs.

Parents Parents of preschoolers, who in today's complicated world need support and advice on guiding their children and responding to behavioral issues.

winning ways

Using This Book

Understanding Preschoolers is divided into seven topics that you can read in their entirety, or you can select a topic that helps with an issue for which you need guidance. Although reading the entire book will give you the greatest insight into understanding preschoolers, each area stands alone as an educational or training tool. Here's what the book covers:

1 How Preschoolers Learn Best

2 Helping Preschoolers Succeed

3 Interacting with Preschoolers

4 How Preschoolers Communicate

5 Helping Preschoolers with Separation

6 Helping Preschoolers Learn to Rest and Relax

7 Guiding Preschoolers' Behavior

Is the *Understanding Preschoolers* Workbook Intended for Group or Individual Use?

Either way works great! You can use *Understanding Preschoolers* as a training tool for use with a group or on your own. Either way, read through the appropriate content and complete the exercises throughout and at the end. Jotting down your answers will give you the greatest benefit from the workbook. If you are in a training group, having a written answer to refer to may help you feel more comfortable sharing your thoughts during the meeting.

DESIGN

How Is the *Understanding Preschoolers* Workbook Designed for Training?

The workbook is designed so participants will

- Experience active learning by participating in discussions, solving problems, applying new knowledge to their current work situation, and getting reenergized about working in the early childhood field

- Connect their current knowledge with the new material and have opportunities to talk about and share common concerns and issues regarding team building

- Gain practical knowledge and tips to begin using in their programs immediately

How to Use *Understanding Preschoolers* in Trainings

You can use this book for a variety of training needs and situations. Here are some examples:

- Group of teachers from a classroom
- Administrative team
- Lunch and learn
- Staff meeting
- In-service day
- Partnership of several programs

- Community outreach
- Recruiting tool
- Local conference

Simply format the questions at the end of each chapter as the basis for a workshop series

SELF-ASSESSMENT

How Much Do You Understand about Preschoolers?

Take the following self-assessment to see how much you understand about preschoolers. The assessment focuses on how to work most effectively with this age group. I think those new to the field will learn some fresh perspectives, and veterans can always use a little reminder! As you read each of the statements on the next page and circle the frequency that best describes your understanding of preschoolers, try to focus on how this information can help you improve your interactions with children. Be honest with yourself. Just because you know that a certain practice is good for preschoolers doesn't mean you always do it. Understanding your current attitudes and actions toward preschoolers is the starting point for improving your role as a preschooler teacher and making sure your interactions are positive and intentional.

1   I help preschoolers learn best by giving them many opportunities to move and many things to explore hands-on.

   Always   Usually   Sometimes   Never

2   I set up preschoolers to succeed by having realistic and clear expectations.

   Always   Usually   Sometimes   Never

3   I have positive interactions with preschoolers by being friendly, patient, and responsive to their needs.

   Always   Usually   Sometimes   Never

4   I verbally communicate intentionally and frequently with preschoolers one-on-one, in small groups, and as a whole group.

   Always   Usually   Sometimes   Never

5   I realize that it is developmentally appropriate for preschoolers to experience separation anxiety, and I respond accordingly.

   Always   Usually   Sometimes   Never

6   I create peacefulness and calm during naptime, rather than rushing to get children to fall asleep.

   Always   Usually   Sometimes   Never

7   I understand that discipline is about teaching preschoolers how to behave in socially acceptable ways and not about punishing them.

   Always   Usually   Sometimes   Never

7 Steps to Understanding Preschoolers

Refer back to your completed self-assessment form as you explore the seven steps to understanding preschoolers. Whether you are on your own, reading and working at your leisure, or training with a group, you'll gain practical information you can use in the classroom and techniques for developing better interactions and relationships with preschoolers. Let's get started.

understanding preschoolers

1

How Preschoolers Learn Best

I help preschoolers learn best by giving them many opportunities to move and many things to explore hands-on.

 Always

 Usually

 Sometimes

Never

Preschoolers' Fascination with the World

When you get to work, do you hop out of the car, collect pebbles in the parking lot, stop to look at all of the interesting things along the way, such as bugs and plants, and then skip to the door? Probably not. We adults are usually more interested in getting where we need to go and thinking about all the things we need to do. Besides, others would probably look at us with a little concern. Adults don't usually skip. Maybe we should. Preschoolers are fascinated with the world, excited about using their bodies, and eager to learn more. If you want to teach preschoolers in a way they understand, you will need to see the world through their eyes—the eyes of a preschooler. Are you ready to learn?

The Amazing Capabilities of Preschoolers

Who are these wonderful little people you are educating and caring for? Working with preschoolers can be tiring at times but so rewarding. Take a few lessons from the children when it comes to the appreciation and excitement with which they see the world. Here's what most preschoolers are like:

Preschoolers want to learn. Preschoolers continue the hunger for learning that begins at birth. They learn best when they are able to touch things and do things. This is called *hands-on learning*. Imagine if you had a new computer or some other electronic gadget and you weren't allowed to touch it until you knew how to use it. Even as adults, we learn by touching things too. We learn to use the computer by experimenting with it, to play the piano by practicing on it, and to cook by trying new recipes. Preschoolers need lots of things to touch, hold, and manipulate in a safe environment in order to learn. If you are often saying, "Please don't touch that," perhaps you haven't given preschoolers enough to do or need to put away the things that are not for them.

Preschoolers like to move. Sitting still is definitely not high on the list of preschoolers' amazing capabilities. Sure, there is a time to sit and listen, and you may need rest before they do, but your program will best serve preschoolers if you create an environment that allows for all types of movement, and one in which you plan for lots of activities that involve marching, singing, and physical games. An active but structured preschool environment that balances quiet times with noisier times is the best way for children to learn. It will help them succeed behaviorally. Most adults like to sit. Working with preschoolers involves lots of movement on your part too, so forget the chairs and get moving.

Preschoolers are excited about almost everything. Sometimes it's hard when working with preschoolers to remember to allow for their excitement about everyday things. You may see a clipboard as something to hold the sign-in sheet, while they see it as a thing with a shiny silver part that makes a cool noise when it slams shut. They may be more interested in playing with the caps of magic markers than coloring with them, so give them a few minutes to explore everyday stuff, and then gently guide them to your plan. In some cases, you can even follow their lead and just let them play with the items as they like, snapping the caps on and off. What's so bad about that?

Preschoolers have real feelings. Young children's ability to bounce back from emotional upset is a lesson most adults can benefit from. Children go from tears to laughter in a matter of seconds. This emotional resiliency shouldn't be taken advantage of, though, nor should you forget that children have real feelings that affect their motivation, attentiveness, and sense of worthiness, just like adults. Most early childhood professionals never intend to hurt or shame children, but you should think carefully about what you say and make sure your tone of voice, body language, and even conversational gestures convey respect and concern.

Preschoolers are eager for attention. Most preschoolers are eager for your approval. They want to receive your attention, do what is right, and please you, even if they don't always know how. Like adults, preschoolers want to be noticed, to belong, and to be appreciated. Some children naturally draw our favor, while for others we must make an effort to give them the time and attention they deserve. Unfortunately, this need for attention is so great in preschoolers that they will settle for negative attention if they don't receive positive interactions from adults. Children who act out generally need your attention even more than the less-demanding preschoolers.

Helping Preschoolers Learn Best

Consider what you just read about preschoolers and think about how you can enhance the children's experience in your program.

Preschoolers want to learn. Preschoolers like to touch things to learn. What can children touch in your program?

_____

_____

Preschoolers need a safe environment that they can explore independently. Do children get many opportunities for free play? How can you increase this time?

_____

_____

Preschoolers like to move. Preschoolers use their whole bodies to learn. What do you do that allows children to get up and move?

_____

_____

Preschoolers need a balance of active and quiet activities. What do you plan that is active? What do you plan that is quiet?

_____

_____

Preschoolers are excited about almost everything. Preschoolers need a chance to explore with materials such as glue and paint before they actually make something. How do you let them explore?

_____

_____

winning ways

Preschoolers enjoy playing with real-life, everyday stuff. What real stuff, such as bowls and spoons, or dress-up articles, can children play with in your program?

_____

_____

Preschoolers have real feelings. Preschoolers are eager for your positive attention. What are some ways in which you encourage children?

_____

_____

Preschoolers can be hurt by an adult's impatience or snappy tone. How can you prevent yourself from hurting the feelings of preschoolers?

_____

_____

Preschoolers are eager for attention. Preschoolers have an inner drive for love and attention. How can you show preschoolers that you care through your actions?

_____

_____

Preschoolers will accept negative attention in the absence of positive attention. How can you give each child more positive attention?

_____

_____

understanding preschoolers

The Development of Preschoolers

Although most preschoolers display certain characteristics in the areas of physical, social, emotional, and cognitive growth, each preschooler is unique; and they all grow and develop at their own pace. Some do so more quickly, while for others, the skills take longer to emerge. Here's a simple list of what you can expect from most preschoolers.

Physically

Preschoolers are on the move!
Typically they can

Run with more control over speed and
 direction
Jump over things
Hop on one foot
Climb up and down playground equipment
Clap hands and move legs in rhythm
Manipulate small toys and fasten and
 unfasten zippers, buttons, and Velcro
Draw with writing utensils and use scis-
 sors with greater control

Socially

Preschoolers are forming relationships with adults and children outside their families. Typically they can

Play alone or with others
Play pretend games with or without
 objects
Play pretend games with a group
Take turns
Share an item
Show empathy or concern for someone
 who is sad or hurt
Show delight for someone who is happy

Emotionally

Since children have such different temperaments, some shy, others hesitant, and many ready to jump right in, this area usually has the broadest difference in children's development. Typically preschoolers can

Separate easily from parents
Allow someone to comfort them during
 stress
Adapt to change in routine
Use words to express feelings of anger
Participate in activities
Play with peers
Smile and appear happy most of the time

Cognitively

In our culture, linguistic development—the ability to speak well—is often what people look for as an indicator of intelligence. Keep in mind that not all children are vocal in a group setting or when they are away from their parents. Typically preschoolers can

Speak so others can understand them
Ask questions
Follow simple instructions
Show a sense of humor
Understand stories
Make simple judgments
Imitate others

Helping Preschoolers Define Areas for Exploration

Preschoolers, with their quickly growing bodies and touch-everything learning style, can unintentionally but frequently cause conflicts: "You touched my picture," or "You knocked over my blocks." You can avoid possible conflicts between children by physically defining their work and play areas. Here are objects that give preschoolers adequate but defined learning and play spaces. Some spaces may be for one child and others for two or more.

- Tabletops
- Plastic dishpans
- Placemats
- Carpet squares
- Area rugs
- Empty plastic kiddy pools

- Large paper plates
- Plastic trays
- Bathroom rugs
- Tape on the floor
- Large sheets of construction paper

Maximizing Learning Experiences for Preschoolers

Are you focused on teaching or on learning? With the best intentions, teachers have a tendency to focus on teaching, which is what *you* do. Instead, you should be focusing on learning, which is what the *children* do. You work hard to prepare materials and get children quietly settled so you can teach them. And to a certain extent that makes sense, because there is so much for them to learn. But think about the characteristics of preschoolers and how they learn. What if you were more interested in how children learn and how they use information than in your own plans and intentions? Can you follow their lead? The goals for your curriculum should be as follows:

- Empower each preschooler to become a confident, lifelong learner and a secure, caring person who approaches the world as an invitation to learn.

- Promote all aspects of development: large- and small-motor, cognitive, perceptual, social, emotional, language, creative, and expressive.

- Nurture a positive self-concept, which includes acceptance of cultural and family background.

- Be free of racial or gender role biases or stereotypes, and encourage children to accept and enjoy diversity.

understanding preschoolers

How Do You Help Children Learn?

Working with preschoolers requires a flexible, knowledgeable professional. Take a look at the statements below and assess yourself by circling a number on the continuum. The first statement on each line is associated with more conventional preschool teaching, and the second statement is focused on developing an environment and curriculum that promotes learning. Where do you stand? Acknowledging and implementing more of the second statements (for example, "Teachers develop learning centers" and "Children are encouraged to be active") maximizes learning for preschoolers.

1 Learning is associated with teacher-directed activities.   Teachers support children's learning through daily experiences.

1   2   3   4   5

2 Children play with toys/do activities.   Children explore/discover.

1   2   3   4   5

3 Teachers put out toys.   Teachers develop learning centers.

1   2   3   4   5

4 Teachers place things haphazardly on shelves.   Teachers create logical, picture-labeled shelving.

1   2   3   4   5

5 Learning and caring are viewed as separate.   Learning and caring are integrated.

1   2   3   4   5

6 Room has limited large-motor and sensory play.   Large-motor and sensory play predominate.

1   2   3   4   5

winning ways

7 Room has few places for children to physically explore.

Teachers create distinct places for children to climb on, under, and in.

| 1 | 2 | 3 | 4 | 5 |

8 Teachers tell children what to do and limit talking.

Continual responsive conversations take place between teachers and children.

| 1 | 2 | 3 | 4 | 5 |

9 Children are mostly soothed and encouraged to be quiet.

Children are encouraged to be active.

| 1 | 2 | 3 | 4 | 5 |

10 Caregiving routines are managed efficiently in assembly-line fashion.

Caregiving routines are valued prime times for learning.

| 1 | 2 | 3 | 4 | 5 |

11 Routines and rituals are based on the school's way.

Routines and rituals are based on children's preferences and families' values.

| 1 | 2 | 3 | 4 | 5 |

Creating an Educational Preschool Classroom

14 Must-Have Learning Centers for Preschoolers

Well-organized learning centers allow children to make choices, play independently, and explore and discover the world around them. Check the learning centers and items that you have in your preschool program, and circle those in the following lists that you need to add.

Understanding preschoolers

Active Play Center

- Inside slide
- Inside climbing equipment
- Balance beam
- Mats for tumbling
- Tunnel to crawl through

Art Center

- Colored paper and water to paint with
- Contact paper and things to stick on
- Collage items
- Playdough
- Markers and paper

Block Center

- Wooden blocks with toy farm animals or other props
- Cardboard brick blocks with trucks or other props
- Large interlocking blocks
- Empty boxes of various sizes
- Foam blocks

Book Center

- Books for children to choose and read
- Interesting places for children to read, such as a loft or an empty wading pool with pillows
- Felt board and felt pieces
- Photo albums of children in class, families, field trips
- Books on cassette or CD for children to read and listen to

Computer Center

- Several computers, if possible
- Child-friendly and appropriate software
- Two chairs per computer so children can work and interact together
- Sign-up sheet and timer so children can take turns
- Older, nonoperable computer with keyboard for dramatic play

Dramatic Play or Pretend Center

- Kitchen area with small plates, cups, toy food
- Baby dolls and toy pets
- Handbags, small suitcases, backpacks
- Dress-up clothes for role-playing police officer, dad, mom, firefighter, doctor
- Theme pretend centers such as grocery store, restaurant, bank

Manipulative Center

- Pegboards
- Toy planes, cars, and animals
- Sewing or lacing cards
- Locks and keys
- Stringing beads

Music Center

- Purchased or donated instruments designed for children
- Coffee can or oatmeal container shakers or drums
- Shoe box and rubber band string instruments
- Xylophones
- Bongos

Nature

- Plastic magnifying glasses and rocks, leaves, or other things from nature
- Magnets and magentized and nonmagnetized things
- Tape measures
- Prisms
- Different shapes and types of tubing and small balls

Puppet Center

- Small finger puppets
- Hand puppets
- Puppet stage with curtains
- Paper bag puppets
- Props for puppet shows

Puzzle Center

- Floor puzzles
- Wooden puzzles
- Easy interlocking puzzles
- I-Spy pictures
- Dominoes

understanding preschoolers

Sand Table Center

- Small tub on table for two or three children
- Large, freestanding sand table
- Cups, spoons, funnels, small buckets
- Props to hide: animals, pebbles
- Broom and dustpan nearby

Water Table Center

- Smocks (children usually get wet anyway)
- Towels on floor to prevent slipping
- Clear or slightly colored water
- Small bottles, cups, and other containers
- Things that do and don't float

Writing Center

- Notebooks, loose paper, index cards, envelopes
- Crayons, markers, pens
- Stickers, tape
- Blank pages stapled together for children to write books
- Forms to fill out, magazine inserts, junk mail, grocery lists

Understanding who preschoolers are and how they learn best helps you create an environment and curriculum that maximizes their learning. Your job as an early childhood professional is to help every preschooler succeed, but are you setting them up to succeed, or are you expecting preschoolers to act in a way that fits your program? In some cases, preschool teachers just focus on teaching, not learning. Sometimes programs do what they do because they always have, not because it's necessarily good for children. Let's face it: a few teachers just do what's convenient for them. Really understanding preschoolers is not convenient or easy. It requires you to plan, work hard, be flexible, and meet all children where they are. Let's set every preschooler up to succeed. Are you ready for the challenge? Read on.

OPTIMIZE YOUR KNOWLEDGE

1 Describe a time when you **unintentionally** hurt a preschooler's or someone else's feelings. What did you say and do to let the person know you were sorry?

_____

_____

_____

_____

2 Name three ways you can **maximize learning situations** for preschoolers.

1 _____

2 _____

3 _____

3 Identify one **learning center** that you will create for your program. What will you put in the learning center, and how will you organize it?

_____

_____

_____

Helping Preschoolers Succeed

I set up preschoolers to succeed by having realistic and clear expectations.

- Always
- Usually
- Sometimes
- Never

Do You Have Appropriate Expectations of Preschoolers?

Do you really expect preschoolers in your classroom to act like preschoolers, or do you often expect them to act like small, perfect adults, ready to sit for long periods of time, listen intently, and hang on your every word? By understanding more about preschoolers, their amazing capabilities, and their emerging skills, you can help them be more successful in navigating the world and its complicated social dynamics.

Think about it: self-control, focus, and staying on task are difficult skills for most adults. Can you imagine how difficult they must be for preschoolers? Most preschoolers are just happy to be alive and are so fascinated by their bodies that running and moving are what they do most of the time. Sometimes it's hard to appreciate the high energy level of most preschoolers. Adults often circle the parking lot a few times just to find a spot up front.

Take a Lesson from Preschoolers

Children are constantly observing and enjoying the world around them. When was the last time you watched a raindrop travel down a window? Most adults, including early childhood professionals, are too busy to appreciate or even see the intricacies of the world. Take a lesson from preschoolers and slow down and watch the world; rediscover your fascination and love of learning. Can you learn to marvel again?

Setting Up Preschoolers to Succeed

As a preschool teacher, do you really accept and appreciate that your job is to guide children to be successful? Do you somehow expect that the preschoolers in your classroom will come to you with appropriate social behavior fully installed, like software in a computer? It's your responsibility to help preschoolers succeed, and success means lots of trial and error, mistakes, repetition, and determination.

Even adults make many of the same mistakes over and over—inappropriate relationships, spending too much money, substance abuse, or what you might consider less significant ills, like speeding just a little, talking on the cell phone while driving, or starting that diet one more time. Don't let your expectations of preschoolers be inappropriate or exceed your expectations of yourself.

8 Steps to Creating an Atmosphere to Help Preschoolers Succeed

Children need a consistent, predictable environment in which they are accountable for their own actions. It should allow for the mistakes and mishaps that come with learning. How can you create an atmosphere that helps preschoolers succeed? Follow these steps:

1. Provide a predictable routine.
2. Maintain appropriate and specific expectations.
3. Be consistent.
4. Offer choices.
5. Give positive directions.
6. Allow for mistakes.
7. Establish boundaries and consequences.
8. Believe the children can succeed.

Preschoolers Need a Predictable Routine

Okay, be honest: When you go to a movie, don't you usually sit in the same spot? In the morning, do you have a routine? Can't get started without that morning cup of coffee or hot shower? Children are the same way. A routine gives preschoolers a structure that fosters feelings of security, comfort, trust, and less anticipatory anxiety. When they know what to expect, they feel more in control and can learn more easily. Here are some tips about routines:

- A consistent routine helps children feel secure and teachers prepared.

- Children understand the sequence of a routine and what comes next, even though they may have no sense of time. Routines for preschoolers should allow for more active time than quiet time.

- Cleanup times and transition times often take longer than the activities you plan. That's okay. Learning is happening all the time.

- Routines and transitions can have special music or songs, but music and singing should happen throughout the day.

- Although routines provide a framework for preschoolers, allow for flexibility too.

Preschoolers Need Appropriate and Specific Expectations

Create a list of simple rules to post in your classroom. Have the preschoolers sign their names or make a scribble as a promise to follow the rules. Review the rules often when they are new, and refer back to them when one is broken.

Sample Preschool Rules

- Walk inside.
- Use your words.
- Help clean up.
- Listen to others.

Preschoolers Need Consistency

Preschoolers benefit from your consistent, appropriate responses. Your consistency helps them see the world as somewhat predictable and teaches them to trust adults in their lives. Consistency builds security. If you break from a consistent response, explain to the children why it is necessary.

7 Ideas for Making Expectations Clear

1 Have the children help you make the rules.

2 List the rules in positive form; for example, use "walk" instead of "don't run."

3 Write the rules on a large poster, even though most children can't read. This helps staff and parents know the rules too. Use photographs or pictures to illustrate the rules.

4 Have children sign the rules to show they agree. Some may just make a crayon mark or scribble.

5 Review the rules periodically.

6 Refer the children back to the rules when they break them.

7 Add a new rule if the children suggest it, but avoid too many rules.

Preschoolers Need Choices

Early childhood professionals often expect children to make the right choices, but so often teachers dictate the actions of preschoolers instead of allowing them to make their own choices. Preschoolers need lots of opportunity to select their options so they can learn to make the right choices now and as they grow older. Here are some ideas for choices you can give preschoolers:

- The color of construction paper they use
- Whether they or you will zip their coat
- Which activity to go to during free choice
- Which song to sing
- Where to sit at snack or lunch

understanding preschoolers

- How they do their artwork; the end result doesn't always have to look like you envision, so allow for variation and individuality
- List three more situations in which you can encourage preschoolers to make a choice:

  1 _____

  2 _____

  3 _____

5 Thoughts on Choices

1 Some children are hesitant or indecisive and may need your guidance to learn how to choose learning centers or activities, especially during free choice or open play.

2 Offer children choices only when choices are possible. If everyone is going outside, then staying inside may not be a choice. Instead, say, "We are going outside. Do you want to play on the swings or kick the ball?"

3 When possible, try to offer only two choices. Instead of "Where do you want to sit?" ask, "Would you like to sit here or there?" and point to the options.

4 Be flexible with children's choices unless they are always changing their minds. If they choose green paper and then decide on blue, give them the blue. How many times have you changed your mind when ordering from a menu or picking out clothes?

5 Realize that children make very few choices and that allowing them to choose prepares them for making greater life choices in the future, such as what job to take. All that from preschool? Sure thing!

Preschoolers Need Positive Direction

Preschoolers need to know what not to do, but more importantly, they need to know what to do. For many adults, it's more natural to tell preschoolers all the things they shouldn't do, the nos: "Don't touch that." "Stop yelling." "Don't run in the room." We tend to tell children all the things they can't do rather than all the things they can and should do. Try to talk and direct preschoolers with positive statements so they know how to behave correctly. Look at the examples below and complete numbers 3 and 4. What two examples can you come up with?

1   No running.      Please walk.

2   No screaming.   →   Use an inside voice.

3   _____   →   _____

4   _____   →   _____

Preschoolers Need an Environment That Allows for Mistakes

Everyone—the children and you—will make many mistakes along the way. Be honest about the things that happen, and approach the children with compassion and redirection. You might say, "I know you wanted the car, but please ask for it. Please don't grab it out of her hand." Help preschoolers learn to talk to other children too. You might help a preschooler say, "You made me mad when you knocked down my tower, but I shouldn't have hit you." You learn from your mistakes.

Preschoolers Need Boundaries and Consequences

Although you want to foster an environment of success, preschoolers will do inappropriate things, such as throw toys, hit others, and not listen to you. This topic is so important that I have devoted an entire chapter to addressing appropriate consequences for preschoolers. (See chapter 7, "Guiding Preschoolers' Behavior.")

Preschoolers Need Adults Who Believe They Can Succeed

Preschoolers need to know that you believe in their ability to succeed. Some children will need more encouragement and guidance than others, and you may feel that success is far away for some children. But if a preschool teacher who is devoted to helping children succeed can't see the promise in every child, then who can? It's the preschoolers who are struggling to gain self-control who need your assistance the most. They can be very disruptive and sap of your time and energy, but there is nothing more important than respectfully guiding them to make appropriate choices. Please have patience and believe in the children you teach—it's very important.

Helping Children Succeed by Avoiding Problems

Early childhood professionals often unintentionally create learning and behavior issues for preschoolers. Sometimes your expectations for their self-control are too high. Use the following questions to assess your environment and your expectations to see how you can make them more appropriate.

1   Children are more likely to run into one another, physically touch each other, and become frustrated in cramped spaces. Do you have too little space? Yes ☐ No ☐

How can you provide more space or at least the feeling of more space for the children?

- Break the children into small groups.
- Use hallways for some activities.
- _____
- _____

What other safe areas can the children use for some activities?

- Hallways
- Lobby
- Outside
- _____
- _____

2   Many children like to run and play in large open areas. Other children may feel overwhelmed and withdraw. Is your open space causing behavior challenges? Yes ☐ No ☐

How can you set up safe partitions or low furniture to create cozier, smaller spaces?

- Tension rods with shower curtains or flat sheets work well in smaller spaces
- Shelving units or other furniture that is sturdy and won't tip
- Plastic traffic cones
- Tape on the floor (avoid string or other things that children may trip over)
- _____
- _____

3 Children need to learn to share and take turns, but when supplies or materials are few, preschoolers may have little to do and begin acting out. Do you have too few supplies and materials? Yes ☐ No ☐

What supplies and materials do you need to purchase or ask for as donations?

- More glue sticks
- Crayons that are sharpened and unbroken
- _____
- _____
- _____

4 Children need a variety of things to play with that are not too challenging or too simple. Do you have materials that are too simple or too challenging? Yes ☐ No ☐

What equipment do you have that is too simple?

- _____
- _____
- _____

What equipment do you have that is too challenging?

- _____
- _____
- _____

5 When children have to wait a long time, they will do something, and it's not usually what you want them to do. Do the preschoolers experience a lot of waiting time? Yes ☐ No ☐

List the times that children have to wait. How can you make changes to eliminate or reduce these waiting times?

- Waiting for snack
- Waiting to paint
- _____
- _____
- _____

understanding preschoolers

6 It's difficult to improve your program when adults are resistant to change. Change is hard for everyone. Are you inflexible? Yes ☐ No ☐

Early childhood professionals can all be a little inflexible at times. How can you eliminate the we've-always-done-it-like-this attitude? What are some new things that you can try?

- Dividing the children into small groups
- Letting the children be more active
- _____
- _____
- _____

7 When there are too many things preschoolers should not touch or do, it's hard for them to resist. Do you have too many temptations for the children—objects and places that are off-limits? Yes ☐ No ☐

What objects are off-limits and seem to constantly cause issues?

- Teachers' handbags
- Playing in the sink
- _____
- _____
- _____

If children are drawn to these things and experiences because of interest and exploration, how can you reproduce them in a safe way? For example, if children want to be active, how can they be active? If children want to crawl under things, where can they crawl safely?

Objects or Areas That Are Off Limits	Reproduce the Activity in a Safe Way
Teachers' handbags	Put out old handbags with wallets and sunglasses and other things in the pretend learning center
Playing in the sink	Put out a water table with cups and containers of various sizes

8 Preschoolers are often talkative and noisy. Too much noise, even background music, can raise the noise and activity level of the room. Is there too much noise in your classroom? Yes ☐ No ☐

What makes too much noise? How can you reduce the noise?

Things That Make Too Much Noise	Ways to Reduce the Noise
Children's music playing in the background	Play music only when children are going to dance or sing
Children's shoes	Have more area rugs that absorb noise from foot traffic

9 Children need to learn to share, but having only one object for a large group of children may cause anger and frustration. Are there excessive requirements for sharing in your program? Yes ☐ No ☐

How can you give children a chance to play with a toy or other object for a reasonable amount of time while giving other children a chance too?

- Use a timer.
- Create a list of interested children.
- Ask the children for their ideas on sharing.
- _____
- _____
- _____

Are there things that children shouldn't be required to share? What are they?

- Blanket or comforting toy from home
- Children's own jewelry
- Child's family photo
- _____
- _____
- _____

understanding preschoolers

10 Preschoolers are active learners who need a good balance between noisy and quiet activities. Do you have long or frequent periods of sitting still? Yes ☐ No ☐

List the times that children have to sit still. How can you make changes to these times so that children have more freedom?

Times When Children Sit Still	How Children Can Have More Freedom
During story time	Children don't have to sit crossed-legged. They can sit however they want as long as they don't bother other children.
During snack	Children can help set up snack, serve themselves, use manners, chat quietly, and help clean up.

Are you setting preschoolers up to succeed? Are you developing a culture that allows for mistakes when children don't succeed? Having a routine and positive, consistent interactions with preschoolers will help frame their success. Your attitude toward preschoolers and the ways you structure the environment and the day define the experience for them. Are you interacting with children in a positive way that conveys mutual respect and appreciation for their uniqueness? The next topic explores your interactions and attitude toward working with preschoolers. Do you think you have a positive and encouraging attitude and exchange? Let's take a look.

winning ways

OPTIMIZE YOUR KNOWLEDGE

1   Name three ways you can help preschoolers be **more successful**.

1 _____

2 _____

3 _____

2   Explain why it is important for preschoolers to have many opportunities to **make choices**.

_____

_____

_____

_____

3   Describe a few ways in which the **environment can dictate** the actions of preschoolers.

1 _____

2 _____

3 _____

understanding preschoolers

3

Interacting with Preschoolers

3

I have positive interactions with preschoolers by being friendly, patient, and responsive to their needs.

- Always

- Usually

- Sometimes

- Never

A Positive Attitude toward Preschoolers

What's the most important thing in the classroom besides the children? *You!* Nothing is more significant than the daily human interactions of preschooler and teacher.

The daily education and care of preschoolers is no easy task. It can be physically exhausting and emotionally challenging. Being a preschool teacher requires coping with a wide range of circumstances and no small amount of stress. Excellence in education and care depends on your continual focus on the characteristics and experience of each preschooler and your work to help children through consistent, positive interactions.

How Does a Positive Preschool Teacher Act?

Who doesn't like preschoolers? If you work in a preschool program, you have to like children, right? That's definitely the first requirement for being an early childhood professional, but having a positive attitude toward children is more than thinking they're adorable, enjoying arts and crafts, and liking the idea of being a teacher. Your positive attitude is demonstrated by your actions. **An effective preschool teacher strives to be**

- Friendly
- Patient
- Kind
- Gentle
- Unrushed
- Available
- Accepting

What would you add?

- _____
- _____
- _____
- _____

Do You Really Have a Positive Attitude toward Preschoolers?

Look at the statements below and think about how you respond to preschoolers. You don't have to share your answers with anyone. Not getting a perfect score doesn't mean it's time to hand in your preschool teacher resignation. Hey, that's the easy way out! You're not perfect, and your thoughts about the statements below may differ from day to day, even from hour to hour. Some days are tough!

Assessing Your Positive Attitude toward Children

1 I enjoy working with preschoolers.

Always   Usually   Sometimes   Not Often

2 I have a high tolerance for a variety of noise and movement.

Always   Usually   Sometimes   Not Often

3 I am willing to learn from children and follow their lead.

Always   Usually   Sometimes   Not Often

4 I recognize and relate to each preschooler's personality and developmental level.

Always   Usually   Sometimes   Not Often

5 I am empathetic to the true feelings behind children's words or actions, even negative ones.

Always   Usually   Sometimes   Not Often

6 I accept all children and have no favorites.

Always   Usually   Sometimes   Not Often

7 I do not compare preschoolers.

Always   Usually   Sometimes   Not Often

8 I make each child feel special.

Always   Usually   Sometimes   Not Often

Appreciating Children as They Are

When you understand how preschoolers typically act and accept each child without reservation, children experience your positive attitude.

Is Different or Difficult Bad?

In his classic study of Masai infants during a time of famine in Kenya, Marten deVries found that more of the easy children died and more of the difficult children survived. Why? His conclusion was that the difficult children were more demanding and therefore received more attention and food. What does this mean for the early childhood field? What does it mean to you? Is a preschooler who is different bad? Is a preschooler who is difficult bad? No.

Responding to Demands for Attention and Approval

Preschoolers will seek your approval and attention. Sometimes teachers tend to focus on children only when they are making inappropriate choices, and preschoolers will take any kind of attention they can get, good or bad. Do you tend to give preschoolers the most attention when they are acting inappropriately? Yes ☐ No ☐

Are there certain children who get your attention only when they act out? (Please don't list names, but talk about your observations confidentially with your group or spend time thinking about this issue.) How can you systematically make sure that each preschooler is receiving positive attention? Here are a few ideas. What can you add?

- Smile at the children.

- Tell them that you like their work.

- Ask them questions.

- Make a list of all the children in the class and check off their names after you or another adult has a short conversation with each child. Do this every day.

- Verbally acknowledge children for making good choices or behaving well.

- _____

- _____

Be Positive

6 Tips for Speaking Positively to Children

1. By reinforcing the positive, you're teaching children acceptable behavior.

2. Pay special attention to your overuse of "No," and "Don't."

3. Tell children what they can do. "Please build with the blocks. You can throw balls outside later."

4. It's possible to be firm without yelling.

5. Realize how much more children can learn if you're constantly reminding them of the right things to do!

6. It takes a lot of practice to think and speak positively, but the results are well worth it.

28 Things to Say to Encourage a Preschooler

Good choice.	Tell me about your work.
Nice sharing.	It's okay to make a mistake.
Thanks for waiting your turn.	You're really working hard.
Being patient is hard.	Good discovery.
Try again.	You're a good listener.
I like your smile.	It's hard to sit still.
You can do it.	I forgive you.
Let me help you.	I'm glad you're here.
Are you having a difficult time?	What a good friend you are.
Don't worry.	I like being with you.
Good try.	Great smile.
You're really determined.	I appreciate you telling the truth.
Tell me how you feel.	You're a good helper.
Well done.	That was a nice thing to say.

understanding preschoolers

10 Ways to Ensure Preschoolers' Positive Experiences

1   **Provide time alone with a teacher.** Each child should have the opportunity for some time each day to be alone and truly engaged with you or one of the other teachers. What the preschooler and teacher do together is not nearly as important as being together.

2   **Offer warmth and affection.** Preschoolers need to be in an environment that lets them know they are special individuals with their own needs, preferences, and moods. Sharing pleasurable experiences with you will foster the development of positive relationships.

3   **Ensure individual care.** Preschoolers deserve care especially tailored for them rather than practices that expect every child to fit the program. (You can read more about individual preschool preferences during separation and naptime in chapters 5 and 6.)

4 **Be consistent.** Your consistent, warm response shows preschoolers that you can be trusted and that the world is a somewhat predictable place.

5 **Teach responsively.** Your responsibility is to understand children's individual capabilities and provide them with opportunities to do something interesting, not just have things done for or to them.

6 **Help children learn from everything.** Every experience is a learning experience. Interact with preschoolers in ways that optimize their opportunities for learning and social interaction, especially during routine activities such as naptime or separation.

7 **Respect each child's disposition to learning.** Your own enjoyment of working with preschoolers and your capacity to show pleasure in learning enhances their positive disposition toward learning.

8 **Provide challenging experiences.** Changing the environment and adding new materials can challenge young children. Observe preschoolers and know when to step in to help children who are frustrated, to praise those who have solved a problem or discovered a new skill, and to ask questions and provide additional ideas for play.

9 **Reinforce socially acceptable behavior.** Positive guidance includes giving children limits to help protect them and others physically and emotionally. Your own positive behavior and gentle guidance help children learn to get along with others.

10 **Establish a connection between home and school.** Preschoolers experience the most positive interactions when you work with their parents to form goals and implement strategies.

Interacting with preschoolers in a way that acknowledges and celebrates individual strengths and skills, promotes self-confidence, and encourages their love of learning and fascination with the world helps preschoolers be more successful. Are you creating a program that requires preschoolers to fit in, or are you creating a program that fits each preschooler? We've covered how you are interacting and communicating with preschoolers. Now let's discuss how preschoolers communicate.

understanding preschoolers

OPTIMIZE YOUR KNOWLEDGE

1 How would a preschooler describe the **way you act**? Ask a child in your care and record the answer below. Does the answer surprise you? Why or why not?

_____

_____

_____

_____

2 Explain the possible **positive learning experiences** that can result for the child, the other children, and you in a classroom that has a child who has challenging behavior.

Positive Learning Experiences for		
The Child Who Has Challenging Behavior	The Other Children	You

3 Name three things or situations in your classroom that you don't typically consider **educational**. For each example, list the things children might learn from these.

1 _____

_____

2 _____

_____

3 _____

_____

understanding preschoolers

4

How Preschoolers Communicate

4

I verbally communicate intentionally and frequently with preschoolers one-on-one, in small groups, and as a whole group.

 Always

 Usually

 Sometimes

Never

How Preschoolers Learn Language

Preschoolers learn language and communication skills by being with adults who recognize the importance of communication, encourage their efforts to communicate with peers and adults, and look for opportunities to intentionally and genuinely communicate with them. Preschoolers learn language not only by being in a language-filled environment but also by direct, personal communication and by listening carefully to the dialogues of others. In other words, preschoolers learn to communicate by having conversations with adults and peers and by listening to conversations, even if they are not participating. Hey, you know those preschoolers are listening to everything you say, especially at naptime, when you think they are sleeping or resting.

Conversation Matters

Communication is the framework for how you interact with the world, form relationships, select entertainment, and really for everything you do. Preschoolers need teachers who seize opportunities to talk one-to-one and in small groups with them. Mastering successful communication lays the foundation for emotional and academic success. Good language skills also help children learn to read more easily.

Speech and Language Developmental Milestones for Preschoolers

At three years, preschoolers

- Listen intently to conversations and understand almost everything adults say
- Are often chatty
- Express themselves well
- Speak in three- or even five-word sentences
- Use the connecting word *and* to construct longer sentences
- Have a grasp of grammar—for example, using pronouns (*I* or *me*), and conjugating irregular verbs like *drink, drank, drunk*
- Recognize many letters, especially those in their own name
- Link language and thought closely
- Start to ask questions, especially "why?" questions
- May still have babyish diction
- May lisp
- May leave out consonants at the end of words, especially *k* and *t*
- May have trouble pronouncing *sh, v, z, ch, j,* and *l* sounds

At four years, preschoolers

- Speak clearly so others understand most of what they say
- Know what they *want to say* and usually *how to say it*
- Place words in the correct order
- Use connecting words like *when, if,* and *but* to form longer sentences
- Like to tell stories
- Talk a lot
- Speak quickly
- May sound insistent, argumentative, or rude, but this is usually just an animated way of speaking
- May be able to pronounce *sh, v,* and *z* sounds
- Cannot usually pronounce *ch, j,* or *l* sounds

understanding preschoolers

At five years, preschoolers

- Demonstrate rapid language development
- Use language to negotiate needs and wants
- May have a vocabulary up to 15,000 words
- Speak clearly
- Can hold a conversation with others
- Describe events and experiences
- Ask what words mean
- Tell jokes
- Use the word *because*
- Remember and repeat stories
- Understand that stories have a beginning, middle, and end
- Pronounce sounds that were previously difficult

The Difference between Speech and Language

Speech and language seem like the same thing, but language is more complex. Look at these simple definitions:

Speech: how your words sound

Language: what you say

Although delays or problems in speech and language may differ, they often overlap. A preschooler with a language problem may be able to pronounce words well but not be able to put more than two words together. Another preschooler's speech may be difficult to understand because of a lisp, but she can put many words together to express herself. See how it all overlaps?

So when should you be concerned about a preschooler's speech or language development?

You should take a closer look at the communication of a preschooler if you see any of the following:

- Often looks blank or does not understand you
- Switches around or omits consonants
- Stutters or stammers
- Speaks little compared to other children the same age
- Rarely makes eye contact with anyone
- Has difficulty playing with others
- Avoids being with others

- Expresses struggle and tension while speaking
- Does not use complete sentences
- Is not understood by others
- Has trouble following directions

If you suspect preschoolers in your class may have delays, observe them more closely, speak to your supervisor, and approach the parents about your concerns. Suggest that the parents speak to their family physician or pediatrician. The doctor may evaluate the child and/or refer the preschooler to professionals who specialize in speech and language evaluation.

Having Conversations with Preschoolers

Sometimes it's difficult to organize your classroom, set up for activities, and watch all the children. Do you find yourself frequently saying to preschoolers who approach you to talk, "In a minute," or "Not right now. Can you tell me later?" If you're like most busy preschool teachers, you probably do. How can you have more meaningful conversations with preschoolers? Start by answering the following two questions.

Do You Really Make Time to Talk?

1 When is the time that children approach you most frequently to talk?

_____

_____

_____

_____

2 How could you organize the environment or make changes to the routine so you could spend more time having conversations with children?

_____

_____

_____

_____

understanding preschoolers

Frequent, positive talking during everyday activities exposes preschoolers to more words and expressions and more chances to practice speaking and receive your approval. These in turn build their self-confidence for further conversation.

Can You Remember What the Preschooler Said?

Without noting the child's name, what was the last conversation you had with a preschooler, and what did you talk about?

_____

_____

_____

_____

If you can't remember any recent conversations, perhaps you need to focus more on having real ones.

12 Ideas for Fostering Frequent and Positive Conversations with Preschoolers

1   **Be available.** Preschoolers don't usually make plans to have conversations. Adults have to be physically available to them in order to stimulate conversation. You need to get on the floor where children are building, sit at the table where children are eating—when you are physically and mentally available, most preschoolers will want to talk.

2   **Be attentive.** Preschoolers are very immediate, especially when it comes to their feelings, emotions, and worries. It's not always possible, but when a preschooler approaches you to talk, do your very best to be attentive.

3   **Listen.** Often teachers' conversations are one-sided and not conversations at all. Do you spend a lot of time *talking to* children or *having conversations with* them? You need to tell and teach preschoolers so many things that you can easily fall into a pattern of directive monologues. Try just listening.

4   **Show interest by following up.** After a meaningful conversation, try to follow up with preschoolers. If they went on a special outing over the weekend, remember to ask, "How did it go?" You may have to keep a notepad to remind yourself of the conversations.

5   **Appreciate each preschooler's unique personality.** Some children are eager to chat. Others need time to open up to conversation. Know each child, and encourage everyone to talk when you are one-on-one, but don't push anyone to speak at circle time or in other large-group situations. Did you know that public speaking is one of people's greatest fears? And talking at circle time is public speaking when you're a preschooler.

Ways to Help Preschoolers Speak More Comfortably

When a child is speaking in a group or in front of a group

- Help the preschoolers talk by using a puppet or stuffed animal.
- Give preschoolers objects to hold and describe.
- Ahead of time, tell them a question you are going to ask so they can prepare their answers.
- Allow children to pretend to be someone or something else.
- Encourage preschoolers to explain what they are doing, such as painting or building with blocks.

What other ideas can you think of?

- _____
- _____

6   **Be sensitive to preschoolers' needs.** If children are hungry, focused on building with blocks, or just relaxing in the reading area, they may not want to talk at that moment.

understanding preschoolers

7 Allow for conversation rituals and individual preferences. Some children may need time to play quietly or warm up to the program's environment before offering information or answering questions. Don't be surprised if the time you want the preschoolers to be the quietest, naptime, is the time they tend to want to talk: some because they can't settle down, and others because the calm of the classroom and the time to reflect may inspire important thoughts to share. Try to create a naptime that offers an unhurried opportunity to share thoughts and feelings.

8 Be in the mix. Play with the children and work alongside them. When you do things with preschoolers, conversations spontaneously emerge and sharing may be less intimidating and more natural for the children.

9 Set aside time for each child. As you know, some children will talk more than others, and you need to make sure each child has your attention and opportunities to have conversations. You may need to take a classroom roster to ensure that you are having at least a short conversation with each child each day. If you have a large class and two teachers, divide the group to make sure each preschooler gets time to converse.

10 Ask questions. Many children need a little prompting or gentle questioning to help them open up and share their thoughts. Ask questions that require more than a yes or no answer. "How do you feel about . . . ?" "What would you do if . . . ?" "Help me understand." "Tell me what happened."

11 Follow the rules of social conversations. Model the basic rules of conversation, such as asking and encouraging a response, waiting silently for the response, listening to the other person's answer, responding to the other person, and asking questions if you don't understand. Learning to take turns in conversation is one of the most difficult skills to master for chatty preschoolers. You might say, "You have talked. It's my turn to say something, and then you can talk again."

12 Appreciate the silence. Just being together, teacher and child, not uttering a word, is time well spent. Build a comfortable relationship with preschoolers by learning to enjoy each other's company in silence too. Silence is not something preschool teachers often experience, so appreciate it.

What to Do about Potty Talk, Hurtful Words, or Inappropriate Language

Potty talk is children's way of expressing bathroom humor and comments about other bodily functions as a means of being silly, seeking the attention of others through laughter, or just experimenting with words that tend to draw adult attention. I know a lot of adults who still find potty talk humorous. *Hurtful words* are just that: words knowingly or unknowingly spoken that hurt another person's feelings. Children use *inappropriate language* because it gives them attention and makes them feel powerful or influential. Sometimes they use these words to gain the approval and acceptance of their group, and at other times they use them to purposely make someone feel bad. Preschoolers often use inappropriate language not knowing that it is unacceptable. They may have heard someone else say it, or know the word is not a good one, yet choose to use it to hurt someone or gain attention.

Quick Tips for Redirecting the Use of Inappropriate Words

- **Make a no-bad-words rule.** At the start of the year, remind the children that bad words are not allowed. Include the rule in your classroom rules and post it for children and families to see. "No bad words. Use words that don't hurt others."

- **Acknowledge when a child uses inappropriate words.** Although you should not give children attention when they are displaying attention-seeking behavior, such as using bad words, you still need to respond. You cannot completely ignore the language, but you can quietly say, "That is not an appropriate word to use. You may not say that word."

- **Try to understand why children are using the word.** Sometimes children don't even know a word is inappropriate. At other times, they know it's wrong to use the word but don't know what it means. And, of course, many times the behavior is deliberate. If you know why children are using the word, you can offer alternatives.

- **Give children alternative words.** If children are trying to make others laugh or just experiment with word sounds, help them make up some silly words or phrases to use instead—for example, "squishy grapes" or "applesauce in your shoes." If preschoolers are angry, encourage them to tell others why they are angry. If they are trying to get attention, assign them special helpers or give them attention when they use appropriate words.

understanding preschoolers

Praise the appropriate use of words. Acknowledge children when they speak nicely to someone else or when they express their feelings appropriately. "I really liked the way you told Sam that it made you angry when he colored on your paper. Thank you!"

More Ways to get Preschoolers Talking

Ask questions. Ask preschoolers questions about past events. Encourage details and descriptions of experiences. "Who did you play with outside? What did you do together?"

Discuss feelings. Encourage preschoolers to talk about their feelings, both positive and negative. Talk about the possible reasons for the emotions.

Encourage imaginary play. Create opportunities for preschoolers to engage in fantasy and pretend play, either alone or with friends.

Connect spoken and written words. Provide opportunities for preschoolers to experience the connection between spoken and written words. Label parts of the classroom. Have children tell you stories, and write them down. Encourage children to find the words on charts on the walls of the classroom or on items in the room such as boxes.

Allow preschoolers to talk to themselves. When preschoolers are talking to themselves, also known as *self-talk,* let them be. Self-talk helps preschoolers focus on what they are doing. As a busy mom, I still use self-talk quite a bit!

The conversational hum of a preschool room is one of the indicators that the room is staffed with early childhood educators who recognize the importance of preschoolers' developing communication and who encourage preschoolers to have conversations with adults and their own peers. Next, you'll learn about helping preschoolers through separation anxiety. Are there things you are afraid of? Preschoolers who are having difficulty separating from their parents or families are experiencing a real fear that requires your attention and compassion.

OPTIMIZE YOUR KNOWLEDGE

1   Observe a preschooler having a conversation, and list three **developmental milestones** the child has mastered.

1 _____

2 _____

3 _____

2   Write three questions you could ask a preschooler to try to **initiate a conversation**. Remember to avoid questions that can be answered with yes or no.

1 _____

2 _____

3 _____

3   A preschooler uses potty talk and inappropriate words to get the attention of others. **Strategize** ways to help the child stop using those words and receive attention in other ways.

_____

_____

_____

_____

understanding preschoolers

5

Helping Preschoolers with Separation

I realize that it is developmentally appropriate for preschoolers to experience separation anxiety, and I respond accordingly.

Always

Usually

Sometimes

Never

What Is Separation Anxiety?

Separation anxiety is the difficulty preschoolers may experience when their parents (or other parental figures) leave them in the care of other adults. It is not unusual for preschoolers to be upset when their parents first leave them in your care. The degree to which children are upset and the ways they demonstrate that anxiety vary greatly. For example, one child may verbally protest parents' leaving yet be easily redirected by you to another activity and become completely comfortable in a matter of minutes. Other children may cry, get angry, or even have tantrums. Most children calm down after a few minutes, although it may feel like forever to you and the parents if they are listening outside the door.

Do Preschoolers Really Have Separation Anxiety?

For some reason, many early childhood professionals and parents seem to have more sympathy for infants and toddlers who are experiencing separation anxiety than for preschoolers. Shouldn't preschoolers be able to leave their parents with little anxiety? After all, they can understand the words *See you later,* right? Not always. How children separate depends on personality and previous experiences away from the parents. For preschoolers new to separation or inclined to worry, separation anxiety is a real fear. Your responsibility is to help every preschooler successfully learn to make the transition from family to school and then back again. You do that by encouraging, being patient, reassuring, and redirecting the child's attention to other activities. Exhausting, isn't it?

Preschoolers who experience separation anxiety shouldn't be expected to get over it. They eventually will learn to function in the absence of their parents. Did you have trouble going off to college or leaving home for the first time? Being away from your family is hard for everyone sometimes. The way you greet the preschoolers and help them separate from their parents can often set the tone for the morning.

What Makes You Fearful?

List one or two things that you are afraid of:

1 _____

2 _____

You may have listed spiders or heights or mice. Probably some people agree with your responses and are fearful of those things or situations too. But many people aren't scared at all by them and may even think you are a bit silly. It's easy to minimize the fears of others, but they are real.

Separation Anxiety Is Serious

Wouldn't it be nice if all the preschoolers kissed their parents good-bye and just walked right in, ready to participate? Sure, but developmentally, one of the most intense things preschoolers are learning is how to separate from their parents. The emotional fear and anguish children experience are real, and you should always take separation anxiety seriously. For children, separation anxiety is really about trust. "Can I trust that my mommy will come back?" "Can I trust that this teacher will love me and help me while my daddy is gone?" "Can I trust that I will be okay without my family with me?"

Developing trust often takes repeated positive experiences, which means preschoolers need your time and patience to help them learn to separate from their parents and feel comfortable in your program. So how do you do that?

Helping Preschoolers Separate from Their Parents

Just like you, children arrive at school in different moods and with different morning experiences. Children who are typically ready to join the group may sometimes be quiet and clingy. Rushing families may not have had time for breakfast, and the children may be hungry. Parents may be frustrated and impatient just trying to get everyone where they need to be. As a mother of four children under six years of age at one point in my life, I remember the feeling. Some preschoolers would rather stay in their pajamas and run around their home. You can't blame them for that!

8 Ways to Make the Transition from Home to School Go More Smoothly

Unfortunately, you cannot change how children arrive, but you can try to help them have a fun and exciting time at school and make a successful transition from family to teacher. Here are some ways to assist children in making the transition:

1   Give your full attention to the children by being prepared. (Find out what being prepared means in the "Are You Ready to Help with Separation?" checklist that follows.)

2   Avoid judging families with children who have a hard time separating. Clingy children don't necessarily result from overprotective parents, and being a bit shy is not a fault.

3   Have enough staff members, at least two, so that one teacher can greet the children and the other can supervise the room and help arriving children find an activity.

4   Create a drop-off area that does not cause crowding and that enables parents to say good-bye to their children easily.

5   Greet children and their family members by name and with a smile.

6   Greet children at their eye level. Stoop down or lean over and look them in the eyes.

7   Say "Hello" in a special way, with high fives or a funny handshake. Children like ritual and routine, which give them something to anticipate and feel special about.

8   Try making physical contact with children who are comfortable with it. Hug them or gently squeeze their arm or shoulder.

BEING PREPARED: ARE YOU READY TO HELP WITH SEPARATION?

It's difficult to give children and families your full consideration if you have not prepared the room or yourself. Take a look at the following checklist, and make sure you start each day ready to greet preschoolers and their families with enthusiasm and attention.

Are You Ready to Help Preschoolers and Parents with Separation Anxiety?

1 Yes ☐ No ☐   I have a written plan listing what children can do during drop-off.

2 Yes ☐ No ☐   I have arrived prepared to work at least five minutes before the children are scheduled to arrive or my shift begins.

3 Yes ☐ No ☐   I have prepared to work by putting away my belongings, finishing my coffee, going to the bathroom, washing my hands, and completing my conversations with other adults.

4 Yes ☐ No ☐   I have set up the room and laid out toys and activities for the children to play with and explore.

5 Yes ☐ No ☐   I am working with at least one other teacher when possible, so one of us can greet children and their parents and the other can help the children find an activity and get settled.

6 Yes ☐ No ☐   I am mentally present.

7 Yes ☐ No ☐   I am ready to greet the children with enthusiasm and attention.

8 Yes ☐ No ☐   I am smiling.

When Preschoolers Arrive

When children arrive at your program, they may be

- Eager to come in and participate
- A bit hesitant and need some warming-up time to feel comfortable
- Convinced they don't want to be here and determined they aren't staying

How Can You Help With Separation?

Look at the following three categories and think about the children in your preschool program as they come into the classroom in the morning. Without listing their names, describe how you help each particular child make the transition from family to school. List ideas for each of the three categories.

The Child Who Is Eager to Participate	The Child Who Is Hesitant to Participate	The Child Who Doesn't Want to Stay

Ideas to Help Preschoolers Separate More Easily

* Have something special from home for the child to hold: a blanket, stuffed animal, small scarf with parent's perfume or cologne, or a laminated photograph of the family.
* Have the child look out the window and report what he or she sees.
* Read a book together.
* Hold and hug the child.
* Make the child your special helper.

* Go for a quick walk outside the classroom or preschool area if you have enough staff.

* Get out a special toy like bubbles or playdough.

* _____

* _____

* _____

Who Needs Your Help?

Is there a preschooler in your program who is having a particularly difficult time separating? Check out the ideas above on how you can help the child feel more comfortable. Can you think of other ideas? Add them to the list by writing on the blank lines.

Help Preschoolers Help Themselves

Like you, preschoolers feel more comfortable when they know what to expect. They are often hesitant about entering the classroom not only because they don't want to leave their families but also because they aren't sure what to do. Many children need directions for what to do and where to go, even though they come to your preschool program every day.

Think about yourself arriving at a party, one where you know some people but not everyone. What is the first thing you do? Head to get something to drink, right? Doing so makes you feel comfortable—it gives you something to do and something to hold. Getting a beverage helps you focus your attention and gives you something to concentrate on and talk about. Getting something to drink makes you feel more comfortable. Make sense?

You need to do something similar for preschoolers. Giving them a simple activity to signify that they are present, that they have arrived for the day, can help them with separation anxiety, encourage autonomy, and contribute to their sense of accomplishment. Here are some simple ideas to help preschoolers help themselves.

6 Simple Preschool Drop-Off Activities Preschoolers Can Do

✳ Place a star or sticker on the attendance chart

✳ Say "hello" to a special pet or stuffed animal

✳ Peer in the mirror labeled "Look who's here today . . ."

✳ Put a sticker on their shirt

✳ Put a ticket to enter the classroom in a special box. (Give the children tickets when they arrive.)

✳ Peek in the treasure box. (Put in a new item each morning.)

The Importance of Learning to Say Good-Bye

Learning to say good-bye is a lifelong process and not a one-time event. Throughout children's lives, they will learn to say good-bye to people, things, and routines. Keep the following in mind:

Preschoolers are each unique. Children's past experiences, ages, and temperaments will all affect how they will deal with change and transition. How each child says good-bye is likely to change as the child moves through different developmental stages. Any of you remember being a little uncertain or even crying when your parents drove away and left you at college?

Tears are okay. Children's reactions take many forms, often happy and sad at the same time. Children may react to change with excitement and enthusiasm, or by sulking, regressing, and even being aggressive. Tears are okay too. Crying is an emotionally appropriate response to saying good-bye to the comfort, security, and even the love we have for people, places, and things.

Think positively. Even though good-byes can be sad, you can talk with preschoolers about good things to follow. Tell them about the positive things that are going to happen: "We'll have fun this morning playing with water, and Mommy will be back this afternoon." Too much talk about how difficult it is to say good-bye can sometimes make children more upset, so take your cues from the preschoolers. Never ignore their feelings, and be encouraging.

When Parents Have a Hard Time Saying Good-Bye

Sometimes it's not the preschooler who has a difficult time separating; it's the parents. You can make parents feel comfortable about your program in many ways, and the more comfortable they feel, the more easily they can leave. Do you make it easier?

SELF-ASSESSMENT

● **Making Separation Easier for Children and Their Families**

Do you make separation easier for preschoolers and their families? Take a look at the following assessment and honestly rate yourself by circling the best choice after each statement.

1 I greet both the parents and the children by name as they arrive.

   Always　　Usually　　Sometimes　　Never

2 If I am busy when a parent and child arrive, I greet them and let them know that I will be with them as soon as I can.

   Always　　Usually　　Sometimes　　Never

3 I am sensitive to cues from parents about being in a hurry. If they look as if they're rushed and I have nothing urgent to talk about, I don't keep them.

   Always　　Usually　　Sometimes　　Never

4 I have the room set up in an inviting way so something attractive can engage the children upon arrival. This helps them make the transition from home to child care.

   Always　　Usually　　Sometimes　　Never

5 If a parent has a concern and I am very busy, I say so and make a definite appointment to talk about the concern.

   Always　　Usually　　Sometimes　　Never

6 I communicate a tone of openness. I display the menu and the daily plans.

   Always　　Usually　　Sometimes　　Never

7 I let parents know when guests or other visitors will be present.

   Always　　Usually　　Sometimes　　Never

8 I inform parents of staff changes and introduce substitutes to parents and children.

   Always　　Usually　　Sometimes　　Never

9 I introduce parents to other parents.

        Always   Usually   Sometimes   Never

10 I communicate the message, "What happens here is your business too."

        Always   Usually   Sometimes   Never

11 I invite parents in to the room to play with their preschoolers or simply to observe.

        Always   Usually   Sometimes   Never

Separation can vary from day to day, from child to child. It definitely demands a great deal of your attention as children leave the comfort of their families. Helping children learn to make the transition is an important part of your curriculum and one that you should plan for and implement with your full compassion, enthusiasm, and creativity. Most children quickly adapt after a period of adjustment. Your job as an early childhood professional is to help children and their families feel welcome and comfortable in your program. By providing preschoolers with fun, engaging, and developmentally appropriate activities, you ensure that they will have lots of things to redirect their attention from Mommy leaving. Continue reading for an interesting perspective on naptime and ways to help preschoolers relax and rest.

OPTIMIZE YOUR KNOWLEDGE

1   Describe **separation anxiety**.

_____

_____

_____

_____

2   List at least five ways you can help preschoolers make a more successful **transition** from home to school.

1 _____

2 _____

3 _____

4 _____

5 _____

3   Develop a plan for a **parent** who is having more trouble separating than the preschooler. What would you say to the parent, and what could you do for the parent to make him or her more comfortable?

_____

_____

_____

_____

understanding preschoolers

6

Helping Preschoolers Learn to Rest and Relax

I create peacefulness and calm during naptime, rather than rushing to get children to fall asleep.

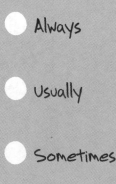

- Always
- Usually
- Sometimes
- Never

Naptime: The Favorite Time of the Day— for Teachers, That Is

After the end of a busy preschool morning, naptime may be the favorite time for preschool teachers and the least favorite time for some children. Why? Children, even sleepy and tired ones, want to keep going, while teachers need a break. Actually, everyone needs a break. All children need time to rest quietly, even if they don't fall asleep, after their busy morning of activity and learning. Naptime can be a time of stress and resistance or one of relaxation and rest. It all depends on whether you're looking at it from the perspective of the children or the teacher. Wouldn't it be great if all adults were required to take a nap too?

What's the Goal of Naptime?

1. For all the preschoolers in the class to sleep as long as possible
2. For the teacher to finally get a chance to sit down and relax
3. For the parents to get upset because they believe naps keep their children from sleeping at night
4. For the children to feel frustrated because they have to stay on their mats
5. For preschoolers and teachers to have a short time of rest and relaxation

As much as all of these answers may be true to a certain extent, you know that the real answer is 5.

My Naptime Story

As a preschool teacher, I loved naptime. Sure, I'll admit that I enjoyed the downtime to work on lesson plans, prepare for the afternoon, and just take a break. And my preschoolers, who were spending an entire day in education and care, needed the break too. Many years ago, when I was a preschool teacher at the United Nations in New York City, the other teachers and I had twenty preschoolers to settle down each day after lunch. Back then, we had the cots with metal legs that were about a foot off the floor. We strategically placed the cots around the room, nonsleepers away from sleepers, and squirmier children and cot escapers near the table where the teachers usually sat to eat and work. On one particular day, after a long process of rubbing backs and settling children, the other teachers and I sat down to chat and work in the room. I always sat so I could watch the entire room of children, and as I quickly scanned the room, I noted the sleepers comfortable and cozy and marveled at the grabbers trying to get their hands on anything they could touch without getting off their cots. Then I realized that one cot was empty—Phillipe's cot. Phillipe was my challenging child. He once stood in one of the small toilets we had, shoes and all, and flushed multiple times so he could feel the water swirl around his legs. "It's just like the whirlpool we made in the soda bottle, Miss Gigi." Anyway, I figured Phillipe must have gotten off his cot and headed into the bathroom for another science experiment. I got up quickly and looked in the bathroom. No Phillipe—my heart jumped. He was not in the bathroom and not on his cot. Where could he be? Now I was worried. I called his name loudly, not concerned about waking the other children, who had taken so long to get to sleep. I was scared. "Miss Gigi, I'm under here." I heard a quiet voice in the vicinity of Phillipe's cot. I went over to his cot, lifted up the blanket, and looked under the cot. There was Phillipe. "I'm sleeping under the cot today, since you said it might rain this afternoon. I won't get wet under here," smiled Phillipe. I love preschoolers!

Naptime: What's the Goal?

Think of your naptime goal as helping preschoolers make the transition to rest rather than having everyone go to sleep. It's like doing an art project; the process is as important as or more important than the product. If you gauge the success and completion of naptime as that moment when all the preschoolers fall asleep, you will be stressed, and you and the children will miss a time of great bonding and one-on-one interaction and learning. Here are some ideas to ensure a smooth naptime process:

- Recognize that naptime helps children learn to shift from activity to rest.

- Realize that learning to relax and eliminate stress is a skill that children can improve at and benefit from for their entire lives.

- Enjoy the routine and bonding of naptime: preparing rest areas, reading books, having quiet conversations.

- Teach children to notice and appreciate the calm and quiet of the classroom.

- Address children's fears, such as noticing and naming shadows in a dim room. Remind them that they are not going to sleep for the night and that they will wake up soon.

- Appreciate rubbing the backs of children to soothe them, not necessarily to make them sleep.

- See the important learning that is happening: learning to soothe or relax to sleep, to not be frightened in dim light, to savor periods of unfocused thinking.

10 Tips for Making Naptime a Success

1   Adjust naptime to coincide with the time when most of the preschoolers are tired. You may notice that your naptime is earlier in the beginning of the school year and becomes later and shorter as the preschoolers age.

2   Have a naptime routine like reading a book or listening to quiet music before the children lie down. Preschoolers need routines.

3   Let children prepare their own rest area with your help. Preschoolers can carry mats, put down their blankets, and take off their shoes.

4   Create simple naptime rules. "Stay on your mat, use a whisper voice, and keep your hands to yourself" should be sufficient.

5   Allow children to have books on their mats at a time of transition. I'll bet many of you read a book before you drift off.

6   Position mats and rest areas strategically around the room so that children can have privacy and less distraction. Some children fall asleep easily, and others may not sleep. Place all the sleepers in one area so nonnappers will not distract them as easily and won't have to step over them when they get up.

7   Let children know that they don't have to sleep, just rest. This eliminates a lot of stress for those who are trying to fall asleep and can't. Ever lie in bed at night and get more and more stressed about falling asleep because you can't?

8   Enjoy rubbing children's backs, having quiet conversations, and appreciating the quiet.

9   Avoid rushing through the process. Sure, you have lunch to clean up, forms to fill out, and afternoon snack to prepare, but remember that naptime is a learning time.

10 Judge the success of naptime not on how many children sleep and for how long, but by your calm and reassuring interactions with the preschoolers.

Naptime Rules

Please rest; you don't have to sleep.

Please stay on your mat.

Please use a whisper voice.

Please keep your hands to yourself.

understanding preschoolers

The Big Question

Will children go to sleep earlier at bedtime and sleep longer if they don't take a nap? That's what every parent wants to know! Remember that nap sleep and nighttime sleep are independent of one another for children ages six months to five years. Children who nap are usually less cranky and sleep better at night. For young children, the complex result of daytime sleep, or naps, is physical, neurological, and hormonal development. Children sleep in the day because their bodies cannot tolerate long periods of being awake. Depriving young children of needed sleep can lead not only to poor behavior and reduced cognitive ability but also to limited physiological growth. Think about it like this: depriving children of sleep when they are sleepy can be as dangerous as depriving them of food when they are hungry. Keep in mind, however, that napping past 3:00 p.m. may interfere with their ability to sleep at night, so turn on the lights at 3:00 and allow the regular noise and activity of the room to resume. This should be enough to gently arouse late nappers. Children who continue to sleep may not be feeling well. Observe them closely and share this information immediately with your supervisor.

Children Who Are Nonnappers, Grabbers, Noisemakers, Squirmers, and Self-Talkers

Note: I have used these napper terms to describe how some children approach naptime. These words are intended to be descriptive and humorous, and I'm sure you can easily relate to these categories. Please do not refer to children by these terms. It is never okay to label children.

All of you have special ways to settle down for sleep, and many of you probably have trouble sleeping. I'll admit that I like to sleep on my stomach with my left leg bent up and my right arm under the pillow. How do you like to sleep?

- Do you need a big bed, or does a small space do?

- Do you like cotton sheets or flannel?

- Do you go to sleep with the TV on, or do you like a quiet room? (Sorry to say, but research shows going to sleep with the TV on can deprive you of your best sleep. Children should not get in the habit of falling asleep to the TV.)

- Do you sleep with socks on or off?

- Do you have a special blanket or pillow?

Preschoolers may also have preferences, and some may have a hard time falling asleep. Consider each child's temperament and accommodate unique ways of resting or falling asleep.

Nonnappers

Some children just don't nap. Have them rest quietly for thirty minutes. Then they can play with a quiet toy or puzzle on their cot for another fifteen minutes. At that point, allow them to get up. Yes, get up after forty-five minutes. Naptime is like any other time of the day; you need to prepare and plan activities for children who don't nap or who sleep only a short time.

Grabbers

Grabbers are the children who can contort their bodies to touch or grab anything in the vicinity of their mats. They find interesting things on the floor— and you thought you swept. They need to touch and twirl and fiddle with things. Try giving a grabber a stuffed animal or special pillow that she can feel and manipulate while she soothes herself to sleep.

Noisemakers

Some children may purposefully make noise to get the attention of you or the other children or because they are bored. Try to sit with a noisemaker and quietly talk with her about topics that interest her as she settles down. Continuing to say, "No talking" to a noisemaker is not always successful. Allow her to talk some and then to whisper. Ever been in a library or other quiet place and you just wanted to yell? That's what noisemakers do. I've always wanted to make noise. Hey, is it just me?

Squirmers

Ever help preschoolers lie down on their cots, cover them with blankets, pat their backs, and walk away, only to find that they have twirled about in their blankets and are moving from one side of the mat to the other? Those are the preschool squirmers. They need to move and roll and fidget until they settle down. Allow the squirmers to get their sillies out for many minutes before you try to settle them and rub their backs. Also keep in mind that some children don't want to have their backs rubbed, and that's okay too.

Self-Talkers

Preschoolers often talk themselves to sleep. They love to use their voices to describe what they are thinking or doing. Allow self-talkers to talk quietly. Some preschoolers make a lot of noise and have a difficult time controlling the level of their voices. Even though you may have a whisper-only rule, some children may not know how to whisper yet, so let them talk quietly.

How Much Time Do Preschoolers Need for Napping?

Who doesn't like a class of preschoolers who nap for three hours? Three-hour naps are unusual, not typical of preschoolers. Preschoolers typically sleep for one to two hours, and the time decreases as they age. Sometimes preschoolers have been going full out and need longer naps, and other times many of the children are chattering away and playing through the entire naptime.

Your responsibility as an early childhood professional is to create a naptime routine around the sleep needs of the children, not your need for a longer-than-average break. Sound harsh? Maybe, but unfortunately I have seen classrooms where teachers expect children to stay on their cots for two hours or longer even when they are not sleeping. That is not appropriate.

How Long Is Long Enough for Preschoolers to Stay on Their Cots?

Most preschoolers should be able to rest for thirty minutes on their cots without a book or toy. Resting quietly is a good thing for children and adults. After thirty minutes, if children are not asleep, you can give them books, toys, puzzles, or manipulatives to play with quietly on their cots. These preschoolers should be able to sit up and play quietly. Try to provide interesting and fun quiet activities that you rotate frequently to help engage the preschoolers. After forty-five minutes or so, nonsleepers should be able to get off their mats and play at a table or join nonnappers in another part of the room or building where you or others can supervise them. Another adult must still keep an eye on the nappers.

When Do Preschoolers Stop Napping Completely?

Preschoolers typically sleep eleven to thirteen hours each night, and most do not nap after five years of age. As their imaginations develop, they may experience nightmares or bad dreams at night, but not usually during naps.

How do you know when preschoolers are starting to give up their naps? Take a look at the list below. Sometimes these indications can make preschool teachers and parents a bit worried. They know children need sleep, and they need children to sleep so they can get a break too.

Signs That Preschoolers Are Giving Up the Nap

- They do not fall asleep easily at naptime.

- They are consistently fidgety and restless at naptime.

- They do not have a late-afternoon meltdown despite not napping.

- Preschoolers who used to go to sleep quickly at night cannot fall asleep at night after daytime naps.

- They nap one day and then not for several days following.

- They regularly play at naptime and do not fall asleep.

Nonnappers Still Need Rest

Even after preschoolers have given up their afternoon naps or have never really napped, they still need to rest. We are a society of sleep-deprived, walking zombies, all caffeined up, who need to rest. Isn't it interesting how many children don't like to eat, sleep, or bathe? Three of my favorite things. How about you? Remember that teaching children to rest and sleep is as important as all the other things you teach them.

Preschoolers need to rest during their busy, active days, and most need some sleep. Although naptime can be a time of resistance for preschoolers and frustration for teachers, try to turn that time of chaos to one of calmness, relaxation, and opportunity for quiet conversations and soothing back rubs. The next topic is guiding preschoolers' behavior. Many books have been written on this topic, and there are no easy answers. I address some practical solutions, and more importantly, your willingness to give them a try and help every preschooler succeed.

OPTIMIZE YOUR KNOWLEDGE

1 Observe a preschool classroom at **naptime**. In a few sentences, note what you see.

_____

_____

_____

_____

2 From your observation, describe an instance that was **frustrating** for a child or teacher. What suggestions do you have to possibly eliminate that frustration?

_____

_____

_____

_____

winning ways

3 **Create a naptime routine.** List the steps for preparing the sleeping space, helping children get to their cots, guiding children who don't sleep, and waking up.

_____

_____

_____

_____

7 Guiding Preschoolers' Behavior

I understand that discipline is about teaching preschoolers how to behave in socially acceptable ways and not about punishing them.

- Always
- Usually
- Sometimes
- Never

A Teachable Moment

Preschoolers are learning how to get along with others, act in socially acceptable ways, function in groups, take turns, and share. That's a lot of learning! Most preschoolers will make some mistakes as they try to master these skills, and so will you. So how do you guide preschoolers when they are acting inappropriately? You guide them with patience and compassion, even when you feel like you shouldn't have to tell them a hundred times. Think of discipline as a teachable moment, an opportunity to help children learn to function well socially and to feel good about themselves in the process. As an early childhood professional, you spend a great deal of time guiding and redirecting the actions and behaviors of preschoolers. Socialization and guidance are huge and important parts of your program and curriculum.

12 Principles for Effective Guidance and Discipline

1. Discipline is not punishment but an opportunity to help children behave appropriately.

2. Discipline includes preventing problems and helping children succeed.

3. Discipline helps children learn self-control and how to get along with others.

4. It is appropriate and necessary for children to be curious, experiment, and test the limits.

5   The environment and routine should prevent crowding of children and other frustrations that lead to discipline concerns.

6   All children, at all times, even at their most challenging moments, deserve respect.

7   Labeling children negatively affects everyone, especially the children being labeled.

8   Role-modeling appropriate behavior is more effective than telling children how to behave.

9   Before intervening, give children an opportunity to work out their struggles themselves, when possible.

10 Limit your use of the word *no*.

11 Having a consistent adult response is the norm for redirecting behavior.

12 Praise good behavior and efforts or attempts at trying to behave appropriately.

SELF-CONTROL, NOT YOUR CONTROL

Discipline is not about your power and control over preschoolers. Discipline, or socialization and guidance, is about empowering children and teaching them self-control.

Perfect Never Really Comes

It's easy to become overwhelmed and anxious when you're in the midst of working with preschoolers, especially those who are acting out. Are you eagerly waiting for the day when everything will be just right, when all your preschoolers will sit quietly and listen to your every word? When you are working with preschoolers, that perfect day never really comes. Are you looking for perfect? Perhaps it's more realistic to learn how to ride the rapids with the children than to keep searching for smooth waters.

understanding preschoolers

Preschool Behaviors and Teachers' Responses

What Makes You Crazy?

It's time to be honest about your feelings about preschoolers and their actions. List the types of behaviors that preschool children sometimes display that make you feel anxious, impatient, even angry. In other words, what makes you feel crazy? Be honest about what irritates you—for example, running around, talking. Remember not to list children's names, just their behaviors.

_____

_____

_____

What Makes the Children Crazy?

What if someone asked the preschoolers in your preschool classroom, "Does your teacher yell and get angry a lot?" How would they answer? Children learn most from your behavior. If you want to teach them appropriate behavior, you must model appropriate behavior. Are you patient and kind or angry and frustrated? Identify your behavioral and emotional strengths. In what areas do you need more growth? List those below.

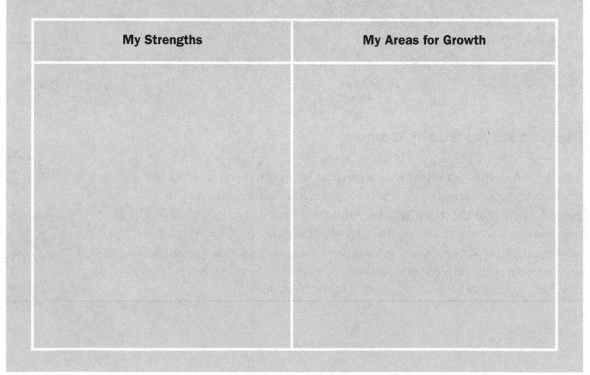

My Strengths	My Areas for Growth

Steps to Successfully Guide Inappropriate Behavior

What Should You Do?

1 Stop what you are doing and go to the preschooler who is misbehaving. In a firm but friendly voice, ask the child to stop. Speak to the child at close range whenever possible, not from across the room. Your tone of voice and your proximity can communicate approval or disapproval effectively.

2 Help the preschooler stop the inappropriate behavior. Redirect the child to a new activity or physically remove him, the object, or the victim, if necessary. Remember, the goal is to help the child behave appropriately.

3 Validate the preschooler's feelings. Always recognize and acknowledge the child's feeling of anger, confusion, or hurt as legitimate. "I know it makes you angry when Antonio takes your toy, but you can't hit him. Tell him no." "It's frustrating when you can't get the toy to work the way you want it to. May I help you?"

4 Redirect the preschooler to positive behavior. Tell the child what the appropriate behavior is and model it. Find an acceptable alternative when appropriate. If you are stopping a child from doing something, don't say what the preschooler cannot do; say what the child can do. "You can't throw the blocks, but you can throw this ball."

5 Give a brief explanation of why the behavior is unacceptable. In simple terms, explain to the preschooler what behavior was unacceptable. Reasons may be obvious to you but not to preschoolers. State the consequences for continued inappropriate behavior. The goal is to help preschoolers make the right choices; however, sometimes you must give children consequences to help them maintain self-respect while learning greater self-control.

6 Recognize your own inability to deal with some situations. Seek help if you are about to lose control or are too angry to handle a situation.

understanding preschoolers

Redirecting Preschoolers with Positive Words

What Should You Say?

I understand that _____

Please (do) _____

Please don't _____

Because _____

I understand that (a validation of the
preschooler's feelings) _____

Please (do) (what the child
should do) _____

Please don't (what the child
shouldn't do) _____

Because (the reason why) _____

I understand that you are
(how the child is feeling) _____

Please do (what is a better response) _____

Please don't (what the child did) _____

Because _____

5 Strategies and Consequences for Inappropriate Behavior

1 **Choices** The child selects from two choices you offer him. Example: If he refuses to sit down for lunch, ask him which chair he would like to sit in. "You have to sit down now for lunch. Would you like to sit in this chair or that chair?" Point out the options.

2 **Redirection** The child is guided to a new activity and can no longer do what he was engaged in while misbehaving. Example: If the child is fighting over trucks, he can no longer play with those trucks. "You're having a hard time playing with the trucks. Let's play with the blocks for a while."

3 Logical consequences The child is not allowed to continue doing what he wants unless he does it appropriately. Example: If the child is writing on the walls with markers, they cannot use the markers. "Please write on the paper. If you write on the walls again, you will not be able to use the markers."

4 Time-out The child is not allowed to do anything for a certain amount of time. Example: If a child hurts someone or repeatedly disobeys you, he must sit quietly for a while. "You hurt Joshua when you hit him. Sit here for a few minutes until you can play without hitting."

5 "Stay with me" The child must stay with you. Example: If a child is hurting other children or disrupting the room, he must stay with you. "You are having difficulty controlling yourself today. You hit other children. I want you to stay with me and let me help."

Guiding Preschoolers' Behavior

15 Absolute Don'ts When Disciplining Preschoolers

1 Don't put preschoolers in the corner of a room. Instead of "Go face the corner of the room," say, "Please stay with me."

2 Don't make preschoolers do something to indicate shame, such as wearing a special sign or hat, or sitting in a naughty seat or spot. Instead of "Go sit in the time-out chair," say, "Let's go for a walk around the room."

3 Don't hurt preschoolers' feelings. Instead of "You should be crying if you treat your friends like that," say, "Treat your friends like you want them to treat you."

4 Don't be rude to preschoolers. Instead of "Sit down if you can't behave!" say, "Please sit with me so I can help you make good choices."

5 Don't make fun of preschoolers. Instead of "You should be in the baby room since you are crying," say, "It's okay to cry. Tell me how you are feeling."

6 Don't single out preschoolers. Instead of "You are the only one who did not set up your cot," say, "Let me help you set up your cot."

7 Don't yell at preschoolers. Instead of "You stop running right now!" say, "Please walk."

8 Don't call preschoolers names like "Crybaby" or "Tough guy." Instead, simply call children by their correct names.

9 Don't shake, shove, or hit preschoolers. Instead, keep your hands behind your back when you are disciplining them, especially if you are frustrated or angry.

10 Don't force preschoolers to sit for long periods of time. Instead of "You sit here until we go inside," say, "Let's draw with chalk on the sidewalk."

11 Don't stop preschoolers from having opportunities to talk. Instead of "I don't want to hear what you have to say. I saw what happened," say, "Tell me what happened."

12 Don't call preschoolers *bad.* Instead of "You're a very bad boy," say, "That was a bad choice."

13 Don't get personally angry at preschoolers. Instead, move away from them if you are angry.

14 Don't say "No" or "Stop that" all the time. Instead, use a positive approach. "Please walk inside."

15 Don't use food, candy, fun activities, or anything as a bribe. Instead of "If you listen on the playground, I will give everyone a cookie," say, "Please remember to listen on the playground."

SELF-ASSESSMENT

Do I Guide Preschoolers' Behavior with Patience and Redirection?

1 I admit my own mistakes as a teacher.

       Never   Usually   Sometimes   Always

2 I do not expect a child who challenges me to always be challenging. I start each day with a positive attitude toward that child.

       Never   Usually   Sometimes   Always

3 I do not judge a child and his family about why the child acts out.

       Never   Usually   Sometimes   Always

4 I treat each child with respect.

       Never   Usually   Sometimes   Always

5 I do not want children to fail, even in little things. I do not say things like "I told you you would fall if you ran."

       Never   Usually   Sometimes   Always

6 I realize that sometimes the child who is most difficult or annoying is the one who needs my attention the most.

       Never   Usually   Sometimes   Always

7 I try to remember that what seems trivial to me may be really important to a child, like a broken cracker or someone writing on another child's art.

       Never   Usually   Sometimes   Always

8 I show children sympathy but then encourage them to focus on something positive.

       Never   Usually   Sometimes   Always

9 I speak kind words to children.

       Never   Usually   Sometimes   Always

10 I expect children to act like children.

       Never   Usually   Sometimes   Always

11 I am patient with children and view inappropriate behavior as a teachable moment.

       Never   Usually   Sometimes   Always

12 I express my own anger and frustration with words, not actions.

       Never   Usually   Sometimes   Always

understanding preschoolers

Relax:
Expect Preschoolers to Act Like Preschoolers

Pick your battles. Decide what matters a lot, a little, or not at all. Preschoolers are learning a lot during this time in their lives. Does it really matter if they talk quietly while they are waiting for snack? Does it really matter if they put the blocks in the dramatic play area so they can make block soup?

Redirect and avoid confrontation when possible. Steer the preschoolers' attention to new activities or other interesting things by redirecting or distracting them when you see them beginning to act out.

Anticipate frustrating situations. Preschoolers are more likely to act out in crowded areas, when they need your attention or seek peer approval, when they are trying something they can't do, and, like everyone, when they are tired. Avoid potential disasters when possible.

Make classroom life simple. Prepare the environment and schedule to minimize frustrations, such as long waiting times, sitting too much, or having too few supplies.

Give lots of praise and encouragement. Children continually look for your approval and satisfaction. They want to please you and to be approved of and accepted. Be sincere, because they can tell when you're not.

Enjoy preschoolers for the wonderful, amazing people they are! Children grow so quickly. Have fun with them every day.

Ideas for Sharing Information about Children's Behavior with Their Parents

1 Before you approach the parents, document or write down their child's behavior to see if changing your routine, schedule, or environment will help the child succeed. (Use the Behavior Documentation Form on the next page as a guide.)

2 Make sure that you are objective and not just annoyed with the child.

3 Reassess your expectations to make sure they are developmentally appropriate—is the child capable of doing what you ask?

4 Talk with a supervisor before approaching the parents.

5 Be positive: look for the strengths and endearing qualities in the child. Ask to speak to the parents in private, or make a special telephone call. These are not the types of conversations to have around children or other parents.

6 Be clear about what you see the child doing.

7 Be prepared with specific examples about the child's behavior, when it happens, and what feelings the child has.

8 Be honest and direct with concerns or questions, but be compassionate and recognize the parents' sensitivities. Do not judge the child or the parents.

9 Listen to the parents and try to understand their perspective.

10 Expect parents to respond in varying ways: anger, denial, tears.

11 Remember that you are trying to help the child and parents, and don't take the situation personally.

12 Apologize if you make a mistake or say something incorrectly.

13 Keep the best interests of the child and parents in mind. Let your pride go.

understanding preschoolers

Behavior Documentation Form

Child's Name: _____

Child's Date of Birth: _____

Teachers' Names: _____

Classroom: _____

Date	Time	Behavior Observed	Circumstances	Ideas to Help the Child

Preschoolers are working hard to figure out how to behave in socially acceptable ways while testing the limits of the world around them. Some preschoolers will test a little more than others. Remember that guiding preschoolers' behavior is as important as anything else you do as a teacher. Take the time to patiently and positively help each preschooler succeed. Preschoolers are just learning to gain self-control. You can help them do that in ways that build their confidence and understanding.

OPTIMIZE YOUR KNOWLEDGE

1 Describe a situation while you were working with children when you were a little frustrated and could have handled it **differently**. How will you act next time?

_____

_____

_____

_____

2 Define in your own words why discipline, or guiding children's behavior, is a **teachable moment**, not necessarily a punishable one.

_____

_____

_____

_____

3 A preschooler wants a turn using the pink marker and takes it away from another child. How would you handle the situation? Write comments down regarding the **most appropriate response** and what you consider an inappropriate response.

Most Appropriate Response

_____

_____

Inappropriate Response

_____

_____

For All You Do

Preschoolers have amazing capabilities. Although they share many common characteristics, including developmental milestones, how they learn, and the notion that routine and structure help them feel secure, every preschooler is unique and special. Preschoolers arrive in your classroom ready to learn. The interesting thing about excellent preschool teachers is that you realize your job is not really to teach so much as it is to set up a classroom and routine so that children can teach themselves.

So what is your role as an early childhood professional in the preschool classroom? It's to understand preschoolers so they can respond by learning and growing. It's guiding children to teach themselves in the most effective, enjoyable, and positive ways possible. Does this describe you? Are you that kind of preschool teacher? You can be.

Certificate of Achievement

This certificate is presented to

_____

for completing the professional development program:

Winning Ways for Early Childhood Professionals: Understanding Preschoolers

_____
In-service hours

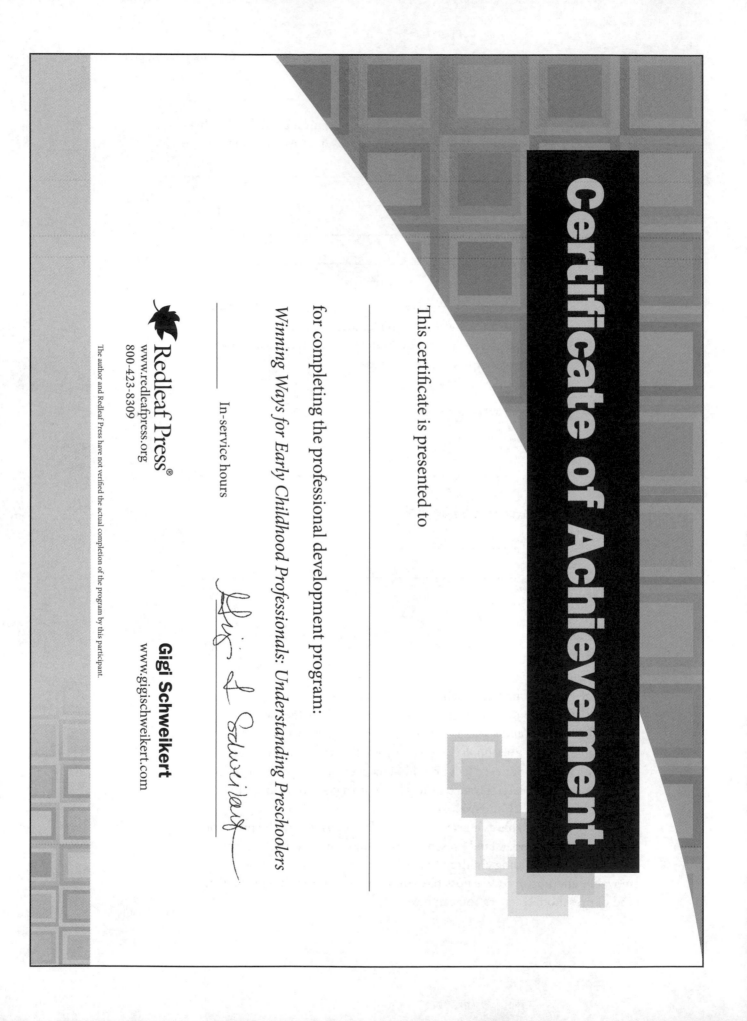

Gigi Schweikert
www.gigischweikert.com

Redleaf Press®
www.redleafpress.org
800-423-8309

The author and Redleaf Press have not verified the actual completion of the program by this participant.